THE OXFORD SCHOOL MUSIC BOOKS

Pupils' Book I

JUNIOR

ROGER FISKE

AND

J. P. B. DOBBS

Music Department
OXFORD UNIVERSITY PRESS
44 CONDUIT STREET LONDON W1R 0DE

First Published 1954
Re-engraved and reset 1964

Copyright 1954 by the Oxford University Press, London

Acknowledgements are due to the following for permission to reproduce songs or music: Novello & Co. ('Go and Tell Aunt Nancy' and 'The Little Pig' from *Nursery Songs from the Appalachian Mountains*); Miss Maud Karpeles ('Sing Said the Mother'); J. Curwen and Sons ('The Drummer and the Cook', 'Billy Boy' and 'Boney was a Warrior'); Mr. György Kerenyi and the Trustees of the Bartók Estate ('Long Chain'); Editions Salabert ('Une Poule sur un Mur' from *La Nursery* by Inghelbrecht); and the Oxford University Press ('Winter' from *Songs of Praise*, 'Puer Nobis', 'Rocking' and 'The Birds', from the *Oxford Book of Carols*, 'The Blacksmith', and 'The New Shirt').

Photographs on cover reproduced by permission of: B.B.C., Fox Photos, P.A. Reuter Photos, Pictorial Press, and *Picture Post*.

PRINTED IN GREAT BRITAIN

J.B.1.

WINTER

WELSH FOLK-SONG: SUO GÂN

1. Win-ter creeps, Na-ture sleeps; Birds are gone, Flowers are none.
2. But the spring Soon will bring Ear-ly buds To the woods.

Fields are bare, Cold the air; Leaves are shed, All seems dead.
Lambs will play All the day; Nought but green Will be seen.

RHYTHM

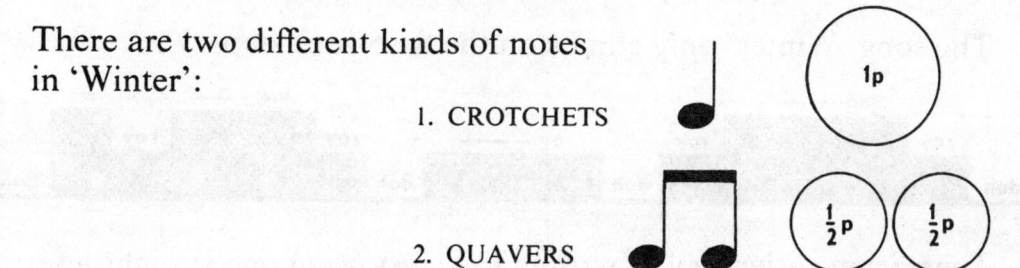

There are two different kinds of notes in 'Winter':

1. CROTCHETS
2. QUAVERS

Two halfpennies equal one penny.
Two quavers equal one crotchet.

Here are three tunes to tap. Which one do you know?

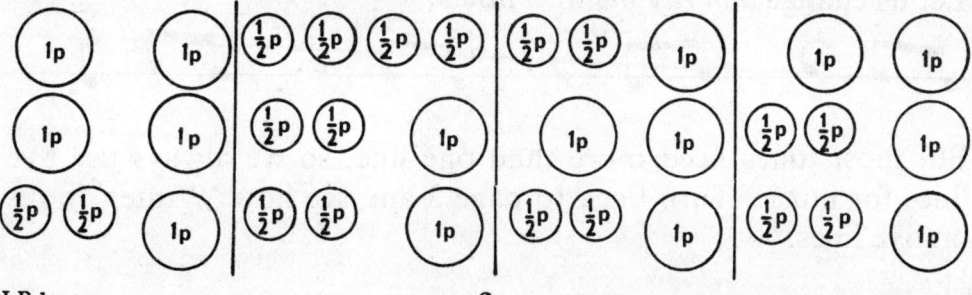

J.B.1.

PITCH

Here is a tune climbing up and down some steps:

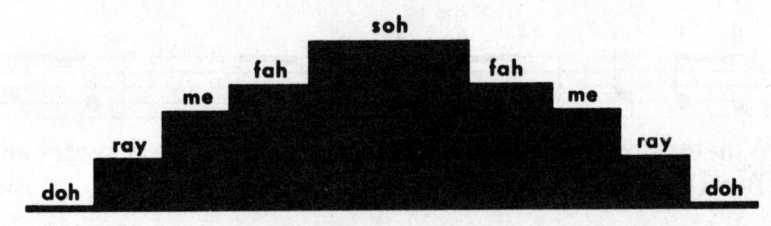

Here is the same tune climbing up and down music lines:

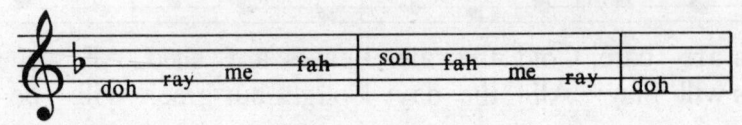

Notes can walk on black lines and white spaces, just as you do when you walk on a zebra crossing.

The song 'Winter' only climbs on the first three steps:

There is an easier way of writing this, just using one straight line:

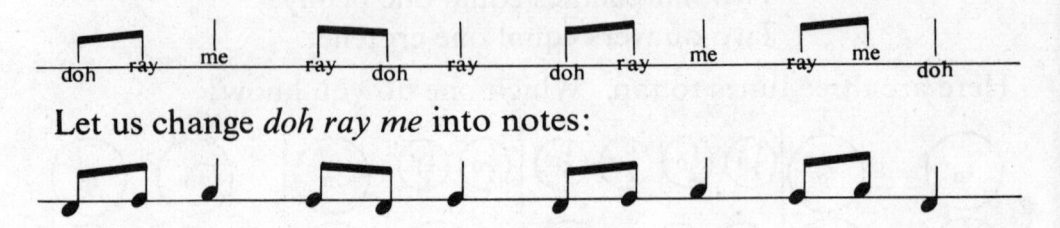

Let us change *doh ray me* into notes:

But most tunes need more than one line, so we always use five lines for music. Turn back to page 3 and see how 'Winter' looks on five lines.

J.B.1.

IN THE SILVER MOONLIGHT

FRENCH TRADITIONAL SONG

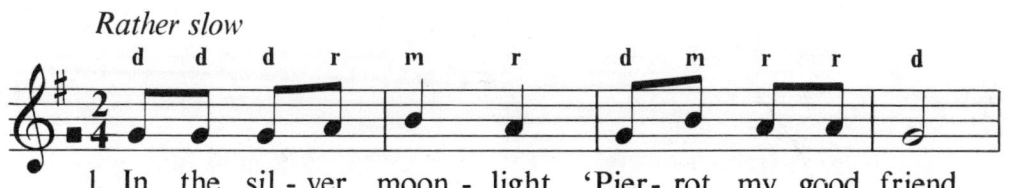

Rather slow

d d d r m r d m r r d

1. In the sil-ver moon-light, 'Pier-rot my good friend,
2. In the sil-ver moon-light, Pier-rot made re-ply:

There's a note I must write If your pen you'd lend.
'Hush, it's near-ly mid-night, And no pen have I.

See, my can-dle's dy-ing, And the fire's no more;
If you need one real-ly, Hark! next door they move;

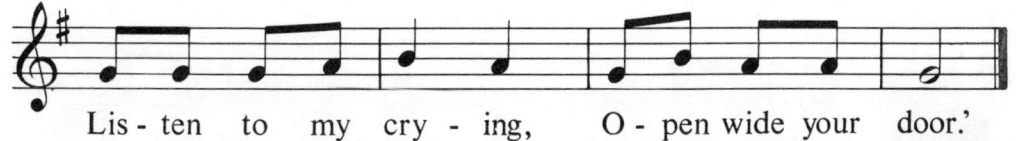

Lis-ten to my cry-ing, O-pen wide your door.'
I can hear them clear-ly Rak-ing out the stove.'

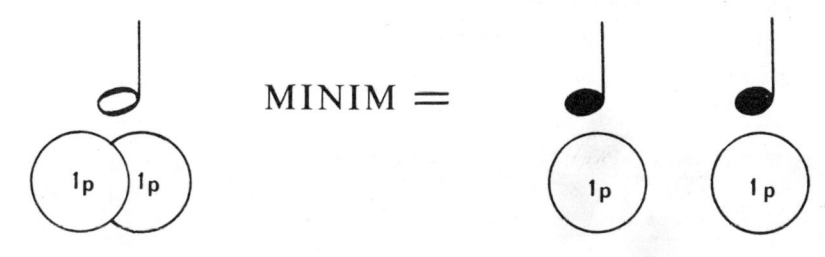

MINIM = 1p 1p = 1p 1p

J.B.1.

ROSIE'S SKIRT

CZECH FOLK-SONG

Ro-sie has a new skirt, it's ve-ry big and lum-py.
But it fits our Ro-sie be-cause she's ra-ther dum-py.

It weighs one, two, three, four, five, six, se-ven pounds,
Eight pounds, nine pounds, ten, oh no, e-le-ven pounds!

REPEAT MARKS: *D.C.*—Go back to the beginning; *Fine*—end.

THE FOUR FARMERS

SONG BY ROGER FISKE

1. Far-mer Higgs, Far-mer Higgs, Far-mer Higgs has three black pigs,
2. Far-mer Howes, Far-mer Howes, Far-mer Howes has two brown cows,

three black pigs, three black pigs.
two brown cows, two brown cows.

3. Farmer Penn, Farmer Penn,
   Farmer Penn has just one hen, just one hen, just one hen.

4. Farmer Hall, Farmer Hall,
   Farmer Hall has nothing at all, nothing at all, nothing at all.

Just after the *Treble Clef* (𝄞) comes a small black square. This shows which note is *doh*. If we like we can put *doh* on the space above. Then 'Farmer Higgs' sounds higher and looks like this:

Far-mer Higgs, Far-mer Higgs, Far-mer Higgs has three black pigs.

This tune starts by stepping up one note and then down again.

Far — mer   Higgs

TIME SIGNATURE: the figures before the first note in a piece of music.

The *top* figure tells you how many beats there are in a bar:
$\frac{2}{4}$: *two* beats (and the beats are *crotchets*).

J.B.1.

THE NEW SHIRT

HUNGARIAN FOLK-SONG

1. Can you find a nee-dle? Is the thim-ble there?
2. Yes I've found a nee-dle, And a thim-ble too,

I shall make a fine new shirt For Ni-cho-las to wear.
I have done the stitch-ing; Now I've no-thing else to do.

This tune starts by stepping from the first to the *third* note and then down again.

Can you find a

BOBBY SHAFTOE

ENGLISH FOLK-SONG FROM NORTHUMBERLAND

CHORUS

Bob-by Shaf-toe's gone to sea,— Sil-ver buck-les on his knee;
He'll come back and mar-ry me,— Bon-ny Bob-by Shaf-toe. 

J.B.1.

VERSE

1. Bob-by Shaf-toe's bright and fair, Comb-ing down his yel-low hair;
2. Bob-by Shaf-toe's tall and slim, Al-ways dress'd so neat and trim;
3. Bob-by Shaf-toe's getting a bairn, For to dan-gle on his airm;

He's my ain for ev-er-mair, Bon-ny Bob-by Shaf-toe.
Las-sies they all keek at him, Bon-ny Bob-by Shaf-toe.
On his airm and on his knee, Bon-ny Bob-by Shaf-toe.

After verse 3, sing the chorus tune to these words:

>Bobby Shaftoe's been to sea,
>Silver buckles on his knee;
>He's come back and married me,
>Bonny Bobby Shaftoe.

Ain—own; *evermair*—evermore; *keek*—wink; *bairn*—baby; *airm*—arm.

The tune starts by stepping up from the first to the *fourth* note.

Bob — by Shaf — toe

J.B.1.

LAVENDER'S BLUE

ENGLISH FOLK-SONG

1. La-ven-der's blue, did-dle did-dle, La-ven-der's green;
2. Call up your men, did-dle did-dle, Set them to work,

When you are king, did-dle did-dle, I shall be queen.
Some to the plough, did-dle did-dle, Some to the cart.

    3. Some to make hay, diddle diddle,
       Some to thresh corn,
       Whilst you and I, diddle diddle,
       Keep ourselves warm.

This tune starts by stepping up from the first to the *fifth* note.

Lav — en—der's blue

J.B.1.

The next six songs are all Christmas Carols. (Not all carols are for Christmas; some are for Easter.) Many carols are very old. Long ago country people used to dance to carols as well as sing them.

UNTO US A BOY IS BORN

GERMAN CAROL

1. Un-to us a boy is born! King of all cre-a-tion,
   Came he to a world for-lorn, The Lord of ev-'ry na - - - - - - - - tion.
2. Crad-led in a stall was he With sleep-y cows and ass-es;
   But the ve-ry beasts could see That he all men sur-pass - - - - - - - - es.

3. Now may Mary's Son, who came
   So long ago to love us,
   Lead us all with hearts aflame
   Unto the joys above us.

J.B.1.

II

GOOD KING WENCESLAS
SPRING CAROL TUNE
Words written for it by J. M. Neale

1. Good King Wen-ces-las looked out On the feast of Ste-phen,
2. 'Hi-ther, page, and stand by me, If thou know'st it, tell-ing;

When the snow lay round a-bout, Deep and crisp and e-ven.
Yon-der pea-sant, who is he? Where and what his dwell-ing?'

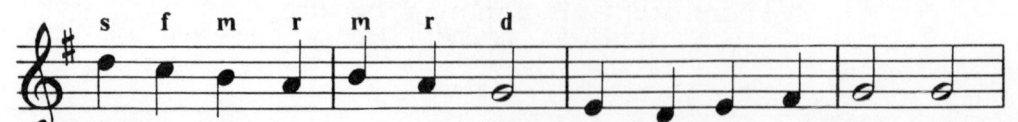

Bright-ly shone the moon that night, Though the frost was cru-el,
'Sire, he lives a good league hence Un-der-neath the moun-tain,

When a poor man came in sight Gath'ring win-ter fu-el.
Right a-gainst the for-est fence By St. Ag-nes' foun-tain'.

3. 'Bring me flesh and bring me wine,
    Bring me pine-logs hither.
Thou and I will see him dine
    When we bear them thither.'
Page and monarch forth they went,
    Forth they went together,
Through the rude wind's wild lament
    And the bitter weather.

J.B.1.

4. 'Sire, the night is darker now,
    And the wind blows stronger.
Fails my heart, I know not how;
    I can go no longer.'
'Mark my footsteps, good my page,
    Tread thou in them boldly;
Thou shalt find the winter's rage
    Freeze thy blood less coldly.'

5. In his master's steps he trod
    Where the snow lay dinted;
Heat was in the very sod
    Which the saint had printed.
Therefore, Christian men, be sure,
    Wealth or rank possessing,
Ye who now will bless the poor
    Shall yourselves find blessing.

ROCKING

CZECH CAROL

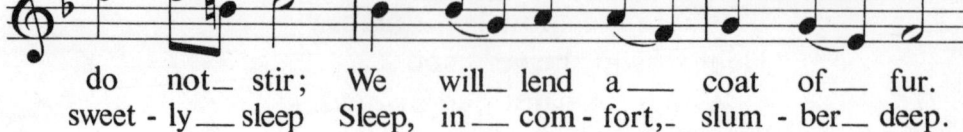

1. Lit-tle Jesus, sweet-ly sleep, do not stir; We will lend a coat of fur.
   We will rock you, rock you, rock you, We will rock you, rock you, rock you;
   See the fur to keep you warm, Snug-ly round your ti-ny form.

2. Mary's lit-tle ba-by sleep, sweet-ly sleep Sleep, in com-fort, slum-ber deep.
   We will rock you, rock you, rock you, We will rock you, rock you, rock you;
   We will serve you all we can, Dar-ling, dar-ling lit-tle man.

This tune starts by jumping on first, third, and fifth steps.

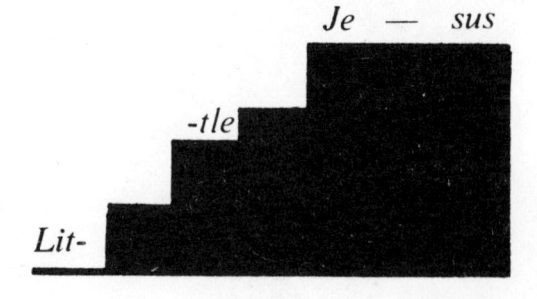

J.B.1.

THE BIRDS

CZECH CAROL

Rather fast

From out of a wood did a cuck-oo fly, cuck-oo;
He came to a man-ger with joy-ful cry, cuck-oo.
He hopped, he curt-sied, round he flew, And loud his ju-bi-la-tion grew, Cuck-oo, cuck-oo, cuck-oo.

2. A pigeon flew over to Galilee, Vrercroo.
   He strutted and cooed and was full of glee, Vrercroo.
   And showed with jewelled wings unfurled
   His joy that Christ was in the world,
       Vrercroo, vrercroo, vrercroo.

3. A dove settled down upon Nazareth, Tsucroo
   And tenderly chanted with all his breath, Tsucroo.
   'O you', he cooed, 'so good and true,
   My beauty do I give to you,
       Tsucroo, tsucroo, tsucroo.'

WE WISH YOU A MERRY CHRISTMAS

ENGLISH CAROL

1. We wish you a mer-ry Christ-mas, We wish you a mer-ry Christ-mas, We wish you a mer-ry Christ-mas, And a hap-py New Year.
2. Now bring us some fig-gy pud-ding, Now bring us some fig-gy pud-ding, Now bring us some fig-gy pud-ding, And bring some out here.

Good ti-dings we bring To you and your kin; We wish you a mer-ry Christ-mas And a hap-py New Year.

3. For we all like figgy pudding, *(three times)*
   So bring some out here.

4. And we won't go until we've got some, *(three times)*
   So bring some out here.

J.B.1.

CHRISIMAS DAY

LANCASHIRE CAROL

1. There was a pig went out to dig, Chris-i-mas day,
Chris-i-mas day, There was a pig went out to dig
On Chris-i-mas day in the morn-ing.

2. There was a cow went out to plough, Chris-i-mas day,
Chris-i-mas day, There was a cow went out to plough
On Chris-i-mas day in the morn-ing.

3. There was a sparrow went out to harrow.
4. There was a drake went out to rake.
5. There was a crow went out to sow.
6. There was a sheep went out to reap.

J.B.1.

RHYTHM

𝅗𝅥 one minim

♩ ♩ two crotchets (crotchets walk)

♫ ♫ four quavers (quavers run)

The *notes* show how long *sounds* are. Sometimes we want to know how long a silence is. *Silences* in music are called *rests*.

A minim and a minim rest (the minim rest sits on the middle line).

Three crotchets and a crotchet rest.

Can you tap the rhythms below?

Which of last term's songs have these rhythms?

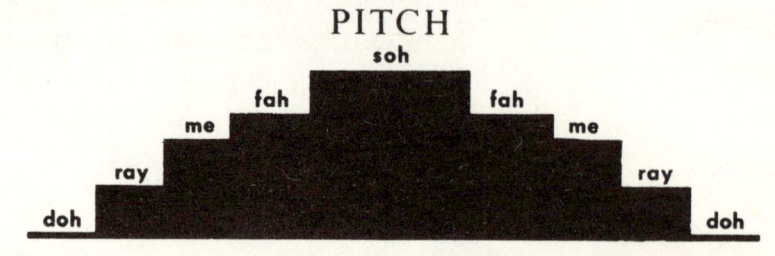

PITCH

Can you sing these tunes?   Do you know their names?
1. *doh me soh soh*   2. *doh doh doh fah me soh me doh*
3. *doh soh soh soh fah me ray doh*

J.B.1.

Which song ended like this?

D s m s r s d

Remember these music terms:

    ⌢   Pause.
  ‖: :‖ Repeat marks.
    D.C. Da Capo, Italian for 'Go back to the beginning'.
    Rit. Get slower.
    Fine The end *(pronounced 'Fee-nay')*.

Here are some time signatures:

$\frac{2}{4}$ Two crotchet beats in a bar. $\frac{3}{4}$ Three crotchet beats in a bar.

$\frac{4}{4}$ Four crotchet beats in a bar.

What time signatures should these tunes have?

E

F

G

Do you know the names of these tunes?

Write down some tunes in $\frac{3}{4}$ using crotchets and quavers.

Write down some tunes in $\frac{4}{4}$ using crotchets and minims.

DOWN IN DEMERARA

STUDENT SONG

1. There was a man who had a hors-e-lum, had a hors-e-lum, had a hors-e-lum, Was a man who had a hors-e-lum, Down in De-me-ra-ra.
2. Now that poor horse he fell a sick-e-lum, fell a sick-e-lum, fell a sick-e-lum, That poor horse he fell a sick-e-lum, Down in De-me-ra-ra.

And here we sits like birds in the wil-der-ness, birds in the wil-der-ness, birds in the wil-der-ness, Here we sits like birds in the wil-der-ness, Down in De-me-ra-ra.

J.B.1.

3. Now that poor man, he sent for a doctorum.

4. Now that poor horse, he went and diedalum.

5. And here we sits and flaps our wingsalum.

THE FOX

GERMAN FOLK-SONG

1. Fox, you must bring back my goose, For I know what you've done,
I know what you've done.
Or I'll set the farm dogs loose And get the farmer's gun,—
Or I'll set the farm dogs loose And get the farmer's gun.

2. Dearest Fox, take my advice, And do not be a thief,
Do not be a thief.
Leave the geese and stick to mice, Then you'll not come to grief,—
Leave the geese and stick to mice, Then you'll not come to grief.

THE LITTLE PIG

AMERICAN FOLK-SONG FROM THE APPALACHIAN MOUNTAINS

Collected by Cecil Sharp

1. There was an old woman who had a little pig,
   It didn't cost much for it wasn't very big,
   A - hoo, hoo, hoo.

2. And that little pig it did a heap of harm,
   It made little tracks all round the barn,
   A - hoo, hoo, hoo.

3. And that little pig, it died in bed; *(twice)*
   It died just because it couldn't get its bread.

J.B.1.

4. And the old woman grieved and she sobbed
   and she cried; *(twice)*
   And then she laid right down and died.

5. And there they lay all on the shelf; *(twice)*
   If you want any more you must sing it yourself.

GO AND TELL AUNT NANCY

AMERICAN FOLK-SONG FROM THE APPALACHIAN MOUNTAINS

Collected by Cecil Sharp

G Major

1. Go and tell Aunt Nan-cy, Go and tell Aunt Nan-cy, Go and tell Aunt Nan-cy The old grey goose is dead.
2. The one that she'd been sav-ing, The one that she'd been sav-ing, The one that she'd been sav-ing To make her feath-er bed.
3. She died last Fri-day, She died last Fri-day, She died last Fri-day Be-hind the old barn shed.

4. She left nine little goslings *(three times)*
   To scratch for their own bread.

J.B.1.

'SING', SAID THE MOTHER

AMERICAN SONG

1. O-ver in the mea-dows in the nest in the tree
2. O-ver in the mea-dows in the sand in the sun

d r m m f m r d r m m r m d

Lived an old mo-ther bird-y and her lit-tle bird-ies three.
Lived an old mo-ther toad-y and her lit-tle toad-y one.

'Sing', said the mo-ther; 'We sing', said the three,
'Hop', said the mo-ther; 'We hop', said the one,

So they sang and were glad in the nest in the tree.
So they hopped and were glad in the sand in the sun.

3. Over in the meadows in a sly little den
   Lived an old mother spider and her little spiders ten.
   'Spin', said the mother; 'We spin', said the ten,
   So they spun and caught flies in their sly little den.

J.B.1.

FRENCH LULLABY

FRENCH FOLK-SONG

Go to sleep, Little brother Peter,
Go to sleep, little Peterkin.
Mother is within, She will bake a cake
For her Peterkin, When he shall awake.

MICHAEL FINNIGIN

ENGLISH TRADITIONAL SONG

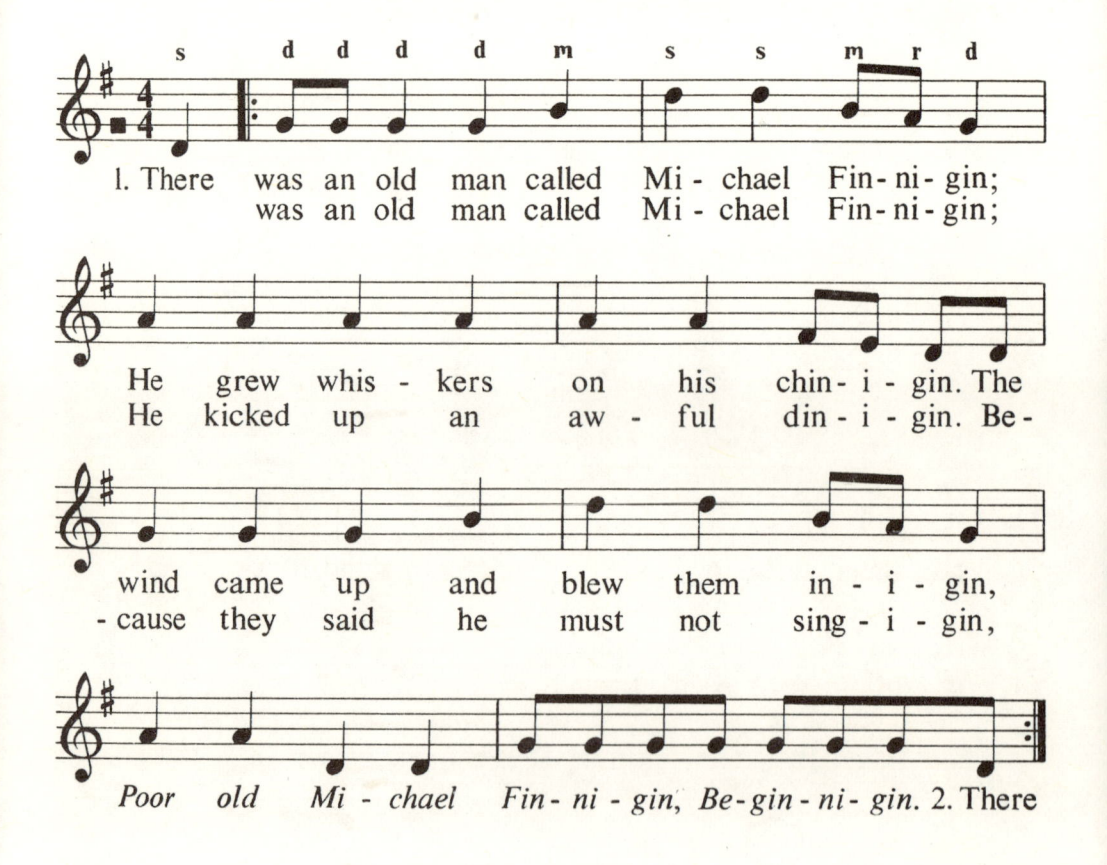

1. There was an old man called Michael Finnigin;
He grew whiskers on his chin-i-gin.
The wind came up and blew them in-i-gin,
Poor old Michael Finnigin, Begin-ni-gin.

2. There was an old man called Michael Finnigin;
He kicked up an awful din-i-gin.
Because they said he must not sing-i-gin,
Poor old Michael Finnigin, Begin-ni-gin.

3. There was an old man called Michael Finnigin.
He went fishing with a pinigin,
Caught a fish but dropped it inigin, &c.

4. There was an old man called Michael Finnigin,
Climbed a tree and barked his shinigin,
Took off several yards of skinigin, &c.

J.B.1.

5. There was an old man called Michael Finnigin.
   He grew fat and then grew thinigin.
   Then he died and had to beginigin, &c.

AH, MY CASTLE FINE

FRENCH FOLK-SONG

1. Ah my cas - tle fine, Ti - ra - li - ra, ti - ra - li - ra,
2. We will knock it down, Ti - ra - li - ra, ti - ra - li - ra,

Ah my cas - tle fine, Ti - ra - li - ra, ti - ra - lay.
We will knock it down, Ti - ra - li - ra, ti - ra - lay.

Ours is bet - ter still, Ti - ra - li - ra, ti - ra - li - ra,
Take our pearls in - stead, Ti - ra - li - ra, ti - ra - li - ra,

Ours is bet - ter still, Ti - ra - li - ra, ti - ra - lay.
Take our pearls in - stead, Ti - ra - li - ra, ti - ra - lay.

J.B.1.

TURN THE GLASSES OVER

AMERICAN SINGING GAME

I've been to Har-lem, I've been to Do-ver,
I've trav-elled this wide world all o-ver, O-ver, o-ver,
three times o-ver, Drink what you have to drink and
turn the glass-es o-ver. Sail-ing east, sail-ing west,
Sail-ing o-ver the o-cean, Bet-ter watch out when the
boat be-gins to rock, Or you'll lose your girl in the o-cean.

THERE'S A YOUNG LAD

NORWEGIAN FOLK-SONG

Fast and very rhythmic

1. There's a young lad up the hill there;
2. I need time to see the snow fall,

With his white coat and his bright hair
Time in Spring to hear the bird's call,

(Piano)

He comes to court me.
And lie in the sun.

I'll not wed him till he's old - er,
Once you're wed there's work in plen - ty;

When my head shall reach his shoul - der
I'll stay sin - gle till I'm twen - ty

Sing twice

(Piano)

And he's tall as a tree.
And— he's twen-ty-one.

J.B.1.

LITTLE JOHN

GERMAN FOLK-SONG

1. Lit-tle John Will be gone Out in-to the world a-lone.
   All his kit Seems to fit, And he's proud of it!
   But his mo-ther has a cry When he comes to say good-bye.
   'I will pray Ev-'ry day; Don't be long a-way.'

2. Weeks fly past And at last Se-ven years a-broad have pass'd.
   Time has come To fly home; John has ceased to roam.
   Can the boy we knew be-fore Be this man out-side the door?
   Sun-burnt brown, Great-ly grown, Will he still be known?

3. One two three, John they see,
   Do not know who he can be.
   Sister says: 'Here's a face
   Which I cannot place.'
   Then his mother hurries in,
   Only takes one look at him,
   Shouts with joy: 'John, my boy,
   Bless you, darling boy!'

J.B.1.

THIS OLD MAN

ENGLISH TRADITIONAL SONG

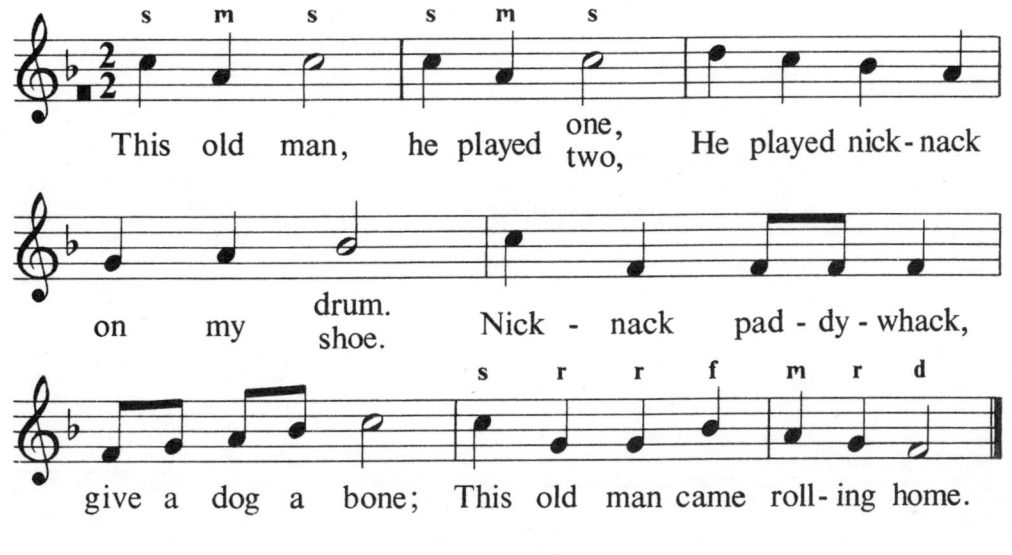

This old man, he played one, He played nick-nack on my drum.
(shoe.) Nick-nack pad-dy-whack, give a dog a bone; This old man came roll-ing home.

3—tree.   4—door.   5—hive.   6—sticks.
7—Devon.   8—gate.   9—line.   10—hen.

THE FOUR LOVES

ENGLISH FOLK-SONG

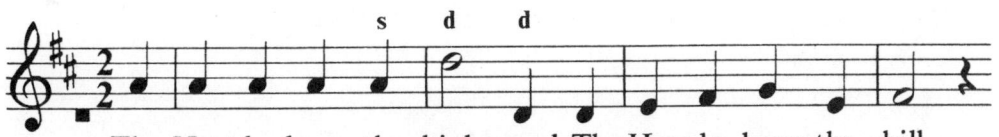

The Hart he loves the high wood, The Hare he loves the hill,
The Knight he loves his bright sword, The La-dy loves her will.

J.B.1.

THE POSTMAN

GERMAN FOLK-SONG

Fairly fast

Tra - ra, the Post has come! Tra - ra, the Post has come!

1. From far I hear him blow his horn, From far its gal-lant sound is borne.
2. O Post-man, will you quick-ly say What you have got for me to-day.

He blows it loud-er still; He blows it with a will,
Which of our dear-est friends To us a let-ter sends?

The Post has come, tra - ra, tra - ra, The Post has come, tra - ra!

3. Trara, the Post has come! Trara, the Post has come!
O wait a bit, don't hustle me,
These letters here, they soon will be
In every house in town,
And all these parcels brown.
  The Post has come, &c.

J.B.1.

THE BLACKSMITH

SONG BY BRAHMS

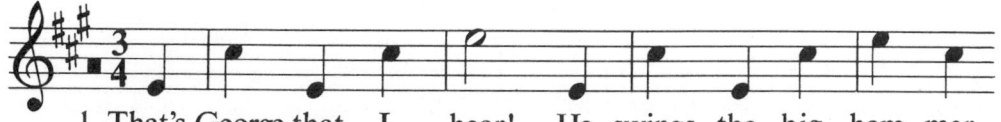

1. That's George that I hear! He swings the big hammer.
2. There in the black forge He stands by the stithy.

The clang and the clamour Keep time with his swinging,
When I pass the smithy, The bellows they roar out,

As bells were a-ringing Through alley and square.
The flames flash and pour out And flicker round George.

J.B.1.

33

THE WALNUT TREE

SONG BY ROGER FISKE

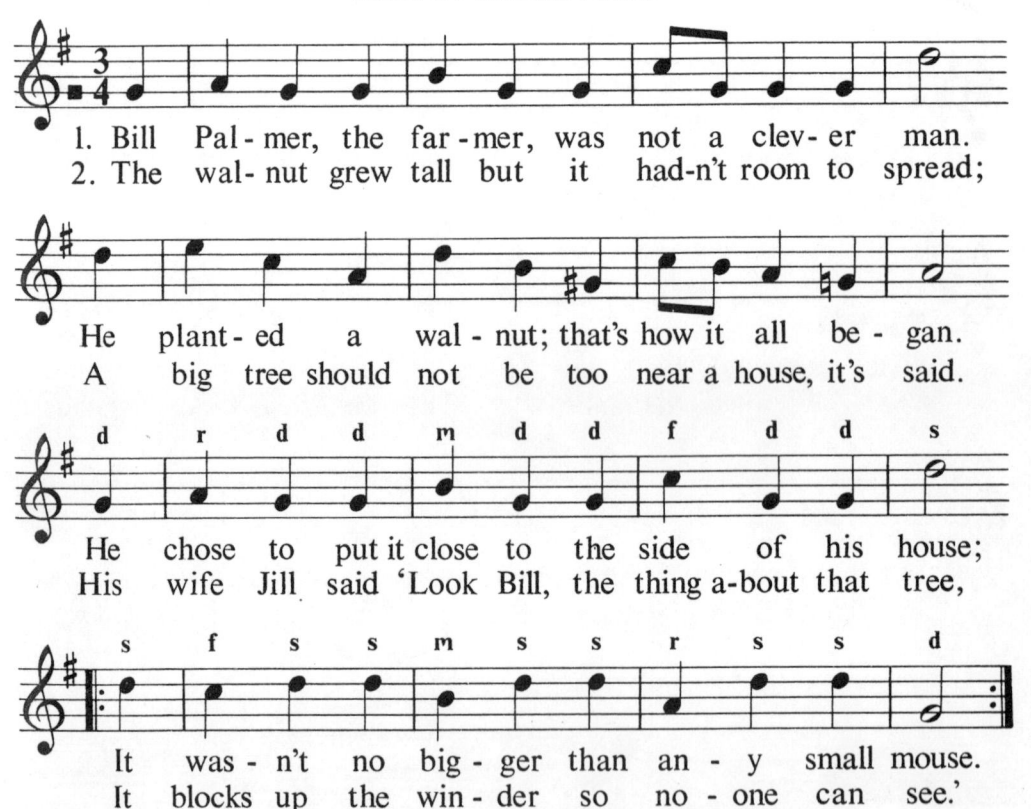

1. Bill Palmer, the farmer, was not a clever man.
   He planted a walnut; that's how it all began.
   He chose to put it close to the side of his house;
   It wasn't no bigger than any small mouse.

2. The walnut grew tall but it hadn't room to spread;
   A big tree should not be too near a house, it's said.
   His wife Jill said 'Look Bill, the thing about that tree,
   It blocks up the winder so no-one can see.'

3. To calm her Bill Palmer said, 'Never mind, my dear;
   I'll climb up and cut off the biggest branch what's there'.
   He had a long ladder, and with his large saw
   He climbed up and sat there; Jill stood by the door. *(twice)*

4. But while he was sawing, his wife said, 'Look at you,
   You're sitting the wrong side of where you're sawing through.
   Oh Billy, you silly, you'll come such a bump.'
   As she spoke the bough broke, and Bill fell down 'clump'! *(twice)*

J.B.1.

THE DRUMMER AND THE COOK

ENGLISH SEA SHANTY

1. Oh there was a lit-tle drummer and he loved a one-eyed cook.
2. When this cou-ple went a-court-in' for to walk a-long the shore,

And he loved her, Oh he loved her, though she had a cock-eyed look.
Sez the drummer to the cook-ie, 'You're the girl that I a-dore.'

With her one eye in the pot And the oth-er up the chim-ney, With a

bow-wow-wow. Fa-la the dow-a-did-dy, Bow-wow-wow.

3. When this couple went a-courtin', for to walk along the pier,
   Sez the cookie to the drummer, 'An' I love you too, my dear.'

4. Sez the drummer to the cookie, 'Ain't the weather fine to-day?'
   Sez the cookie to the drummer, 'Is that all ye got to say?'

5. Sez the drummer to the cookie, 'Will I buy the weddin' ring?'
   Sez the cookie, 'Now you're talkin'. That would be the very thing.'

6. Sez the drummer to the cookie, 'Will ye name the weddin' day?'
   Sez the cookie, 'We'll be married in the merry month o' May.'

J.B.1.

HUSH-A-BYE DARLING

GAELIC LULLABY

1. Hush-a-by darling and hush-a-by dear-o,
   Hush-a-by, darling will yet be a hero.
   None will be bigger or braver or stronger;
   Lullaby little one, crying no longer.

2. Lullaby little one, bonny wee baby,
   He'll be a hero and fight for us, maybe.
   Cattle and horses and sheep will his prey be;
   None will be bolder or braver than baby.

3. Softly and silently eyelids are closing;
   Dearest wee jewel, so gently he's dozing.
   Softly he's resting, by slumber o'ertaken;
   Soundly he's sleeping and sweetly he'll waken.

This song used to be sung by mothers to their babies in the north of Scotland. Many people there speak what is called Gaelic. The words of this song have been translated from Gaelic into English.

J.B.1.

KELVIN GROVE

SCOTS SONG

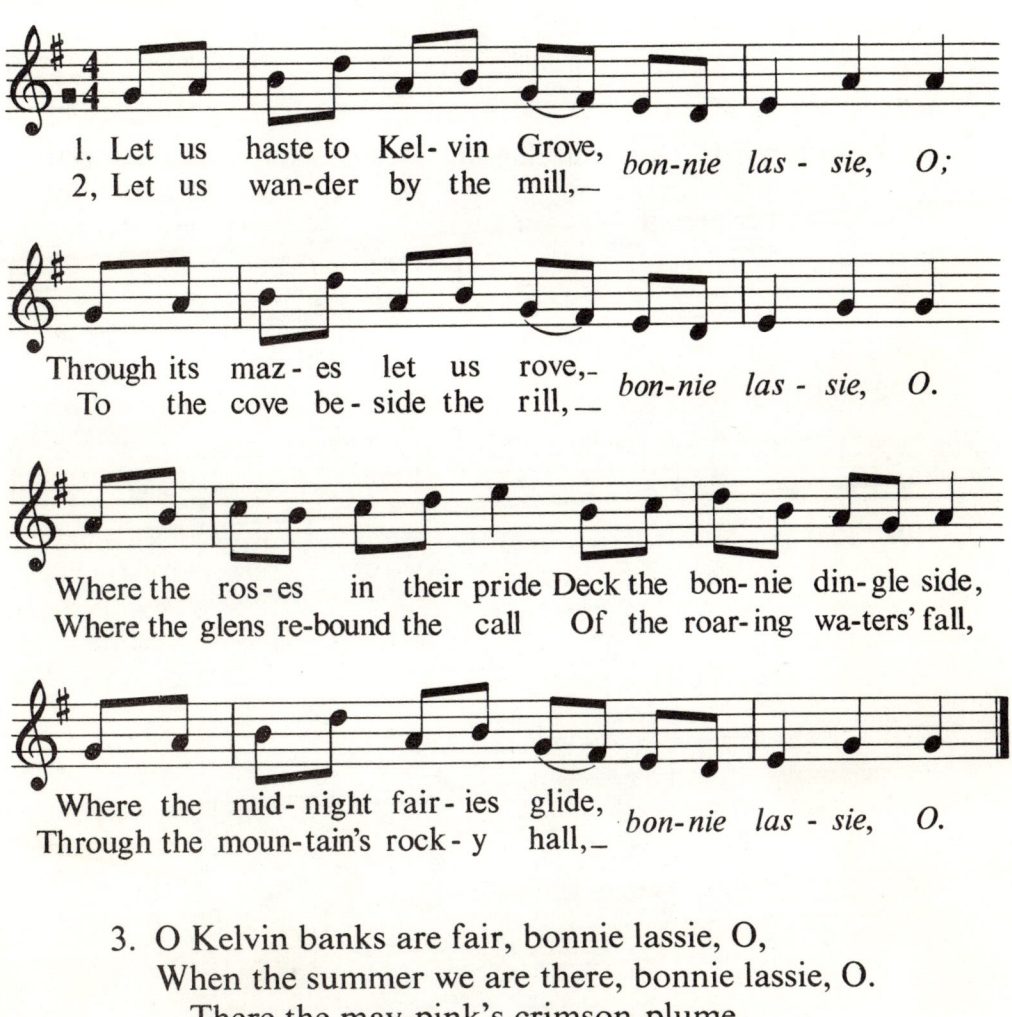

1. Let us haste to Kelvin Grove, bonnie lassie, O;
2. Let us wander by the mill,— bonnie lassie, O.

Through its mazes let us rove,— bonnie lassie, O;
To the cove beside the rill,— bonnie lassie, O.

Where the roses in their pride Deck the bonnie dingle side,
Where the glens rebound the call Of the roaring waters' fall,

Where the midnight fairies glide, bonnie lassie, O.
Through the mountain's rocky hall,— bonnie lassie, O.

3. O Kelvin banks are fair, bonnie lassie, O,
   When the summer we are there, bonnie lassie, O.
       There the may-pink's crimson plume
       Throws a soft but sweet perfume
   Round the yellow banks o' broom, bonnie lassie, O.

PLAYING GIANTS

FOLK-SONG FROM ICELAND

Fairly quickly

Out-side all the chil-dren play-ing gi-ants shout with glad-ness.

Will you please, oh mo-ther dear Let me join them all out there?

How I long, oh how I long to run a-way from sad-ness.

J.B.1.

THE GIRL WHO LIKED DANCING

SWEDISH FOLK-SONG

1. There once was a girl who liked to go danc-ing all day;
2. He said 'I am tied so tight-ly, my hand is quite sore;

She wished to be sure her part-ner would not slip a-way.
I beg you to loose the band just a lit-tle bit more.'

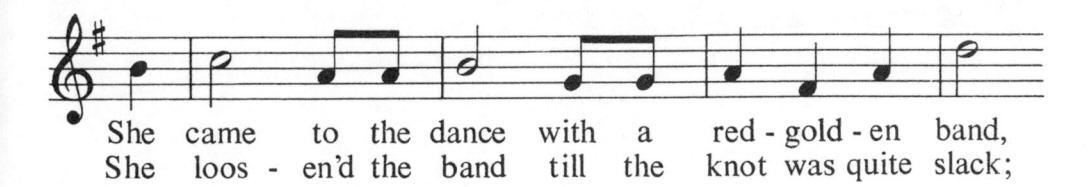

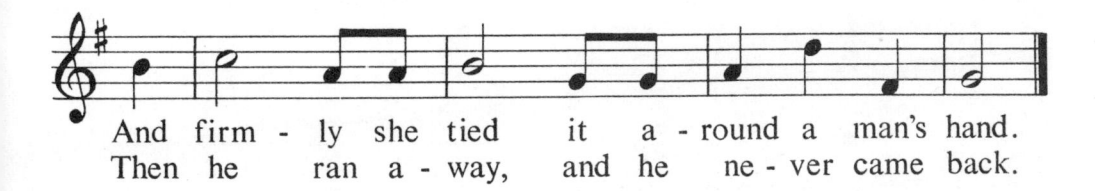

She came to the dance with a red-gold-en band,
She loos-en'd the band till the knot was quite slack;

And firm-ly she tied it a-round a man's hand.
Then he ran a-way, and he ne-ver came back.

THE JACKET AND PETTICOAT

ENGLISH FOLK-SONG

1. As I went by my little pig sty,
   I saw my petticoat hanging to dry;
   Hanging to dry, hanging to dry,
   Hanging to dry, hanging to dry,
   I saw my petticoat hanging to dry.

2. I took off my jacket and hung it close by,
   To bear my petticoat company;
   Company, company,
   Company, company,
   To bear my petticoat company.

3. The wind blew high, and down they both fell,
   My jacket and petticoat into the well.

4. 'Oh, Oh', says jacket, 'we shall be drowned.'
   'No, no' says petticoat, 'we shall be found.'

5. The miller passed by; they gave a great shout,
   He put in his hand and he pulled them both out.

LONG CHAIN

HUNGARIAN FOLK-SONG

Long chain, cot-ton chain, cot-ton chain,
Whe-ther silk or cot-ton we will still re-main a strong chain.
Coins, coins, spin-ning bright in the light;
Ma-ry, turn round to the right light-ly like a fair-y.

Sing twice

BONEY WAS A WARRIOR

ENGLISH HALLIARDS SHANTY

1. Bo-ney was a war-ri-or, Way-ay-yah!
2. Bo-ney went to Wa-ter-loo,

Bo-ney was a war-ri-or, John France-wah!
Bo-ney went to Wa-ter-loo,

3. Boney was defeated. *(twice)*

4. Boney he was sent away,
   'Way to St. Helena.

5. Boney broke his heart and died. *(twice)*

'Boney' was the name people in England used to call the great French general Napoleon Bonaparte.

J.B.1.

BILLY BOY

NORTHUMBERLAND CAPSTAN SHANTY

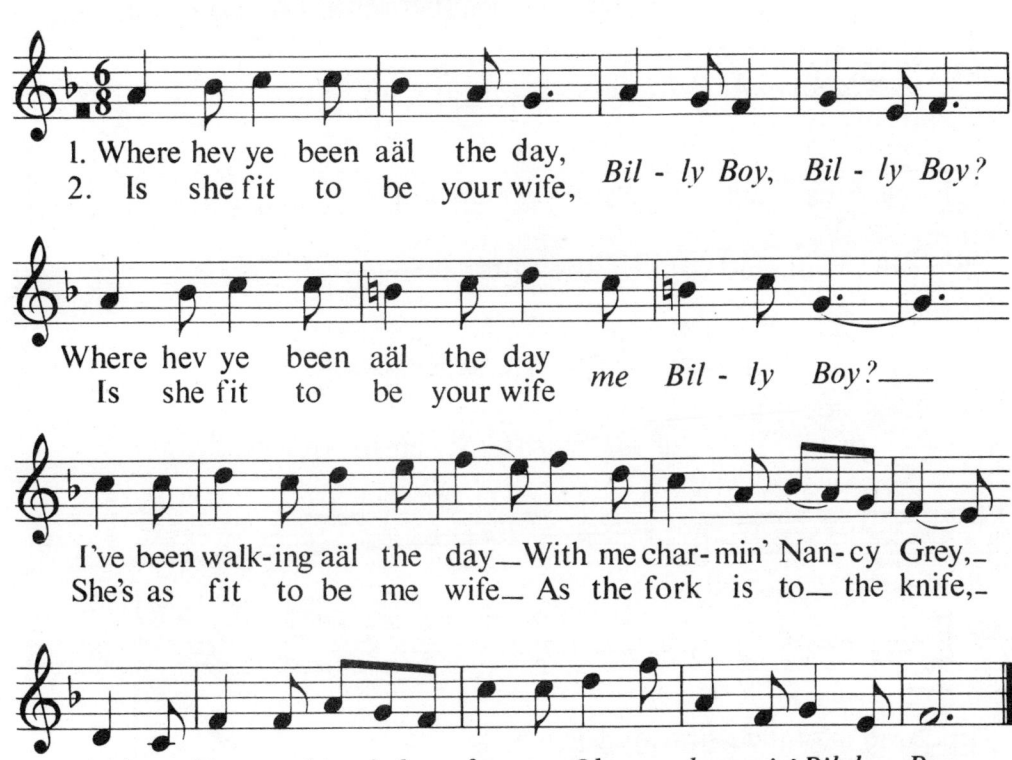

1. Where hev ye been aäl the day, Bil-ly Boy, Bil-ly Boy?
   Where hev ye been aäl the day me Bil-ly Boy?
   I've been walking aäl the day— With me char-min' Nan-cy Grey,—
   And me Nan-cy kit-tled me fan-cy, Oh me char-min' Bil-ly Boy.

2. Is she fit to be your wife, Billy Boy, Billy Boy?
   Is she fit to be your wife me Billy Boy?
   She's as fit to be me wife— As the fork is to— the knife,—
   And me Nancy, &c.

3. Can she cook a bit o'steak,
   Billy Boy, Billy Boy?
   Can she cook a bit o'steak, me Billy Boy?
   She can cook a bit o' steak,
   Aye, and myek a gairdle cake,
   And me Nancy, &c.

kittled—tickled; *myek a gairdle cake*—make a girdle cake.

Here are some French tunes that you can sing to sol-fa. They have been made into piano pieces by the French composer Inghelbrecht, and arranged for orchestra by an Englishman, Gordon Jacob.

Ballade du Petit Jésus (Song for the Baby Jesus)

This tune is played first by the flute:

Une Poule sur un Mur (Chicken on the Wall)

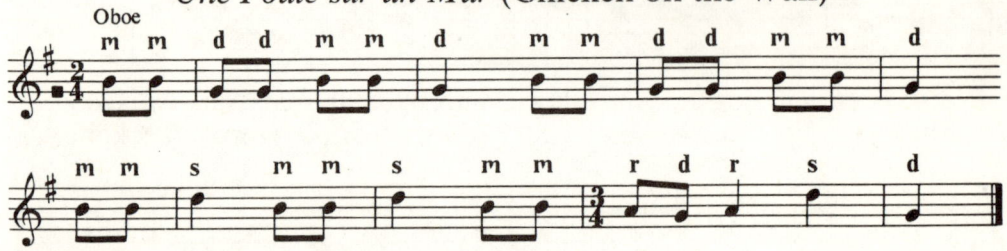

This tune is played first by the oboe:

Here is another oboe tune:

Petit Papa (Little Father)

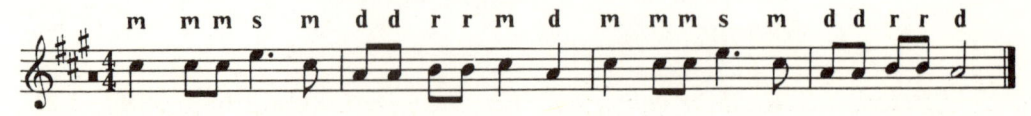

On page 27 there is a French song which Inghelbrecht also arranged.

J.B.1.

There are many instruments in an orchestra, too many to learn about all at once. Here are three of the most important:

Trumpet

The trumpet is a *brass* instrument and can be played very loudly. Here is a trumpet tune by Handel, a German composer who lived most of his life in London, the minuet from his *Fireworks Music*.

Violin

The violin is a *stringed* instrument; it has four strings which can be played with a *bow* (as in the drawing) or plucked with the fingers. (This is called playing *pizzicato*.) In an orchestra there are often twenty or thirty violins; one violinist would not make enough sound. Here is a violin tune by Handel.

Flute

The flute is a *woodwind* instrument; the player blows across a hole at one end of his wooden tube. (But some flutes are made of silver.) Here is a flute tune by Loeillet, a Frenchman who was living in London when Handel arrived.

J.B.1.

Here is an English dance tune called 'Newcastle', played by trumpet, violin, and flute in turn: